A Spider's Life

by
Ellen Lawrence

Consultants:

Suzy Gazlay, MA
Recipient, Presidential Award for Excellence in Science Teaching

Brian V. Brown
Curator, Entomology Section, Natural History Museum of Los Angeles County

Kimberly Brenneman, PhD
National Institute for Early Education Research, Rutgers University, New Brunswick, New Jersey

BEARPORT
PUBLISHING

NEW YORK, NEW YORK

Credits

Cover, © Tomatito/Shutterstock; 2, © Superstock; 4, © Ronen/Shutterstock; 5, © Kaldari/Wikipedia Creative Commons; 6, © Nature's Images/Science Photo Library; 7, © E. R. Degginger/Photo Researchers, Inc./Science Photo Library; 8, © Jeffrey S. Burcher; 9, © Dwight Kuhn Photography; 10, © Josh Kouri 2011; 11, © Jeffrey S. Burcher; 12, © Josh Kouri 2011; 13, © Stevie Ellis; 14, © Edward L. Snow/Photoshot. com; 15, © Opoterser/Wikipedia Creative Commons; 16–17, © Dwight Kuhn Photography; 18, © Jeff Trei; 19, © Cathy Keifer/Shutterstock; 20, © Cletus Lee; 21, © Scott Linstead/Minden Pictures/FLPA; 22T, © Dwight Kuhn Photography; 22B, © Jack Chabraszewski/iStock Photo; 23TL, © Tomatito/Shutterstock; 23TC, © Jeff Trei; 23TR, © Serg64/Shutterstock; 23BL, © Opoterser/Wikipedia Creative Commons; 23BL, © Kaldari/Wikipedia Creative Commons; 23BC, © Ron Rowan Photography/Shutterstock; 23BR, © Nature's Images/Science Photo Library.

Publisher: Kenn Goin
Editorial Director: Adam Siegel
Creative Director: Spencer Brinker
Design: Alix Wood
Editor: Mark J. Sachner
Photo Researcher: Ruby Tuesday Books Ltd

Library of Congress Cataloging-in-Publication Data

Lawrence, Ellen, 1967–
  A spider's life / by Ellen Lawrence.
      p. cm. — (Animal diaries: Life cycles)
  Includes bibliographical references and index.
  ISBN-13: 978-1-61772-414-5 (library binding)
  ISBN-10: 1-61772-414-9 (library binding)
  I. Spiders—Life cycles—Juvenile literature. I. Title.
  QL458.4.L39 2012
  595.4'4—dc23
                          2011044055

For more information, write to Bearport Publishing Company, Inc., 45 West 21st Street, Suite 3B, New York, New York 10010. Printed in the United States of America in North Mankato, Minnesota.

10 9 8 7 6 5 4 3 2 1

Contents

A Dancing Spider!

Today, I used my magnifying glass to watch a male and a female jumping spider on a leaf.

The male spider waved his legs in the air.

He scampered from side to side in front of the female.

It looked like he was dancing!

Mom said the male spider was showing off so the female would **mate** with him.

Ella

I've drawn some life-size jumping spiders. Females are bigger than males!

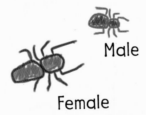

Male

Female

exoskeleton

eyes

Spiders have eight legs and eight eyes. They don't have bones inside their bodies. Instead, they have a hard covering called an **exoskeleton**.

leg

jumping spider

Use a magnifying glass to get a close-up look at spiders in your backyard or in a park. Don't touch or disturb the little animals you spot.

5

Date: June 1

Spider Eggs

It's been five days since the spiders mated.

Today, the female spider laid her eggs.

She made a **silk** covering, called an egg sac, to keep them safe.

The spider used silk from inside her body to make the sac.

Then she made a silk nest in the corner of our porch.

Inside the nest, the spider is guarding her egg sac.

egg sac

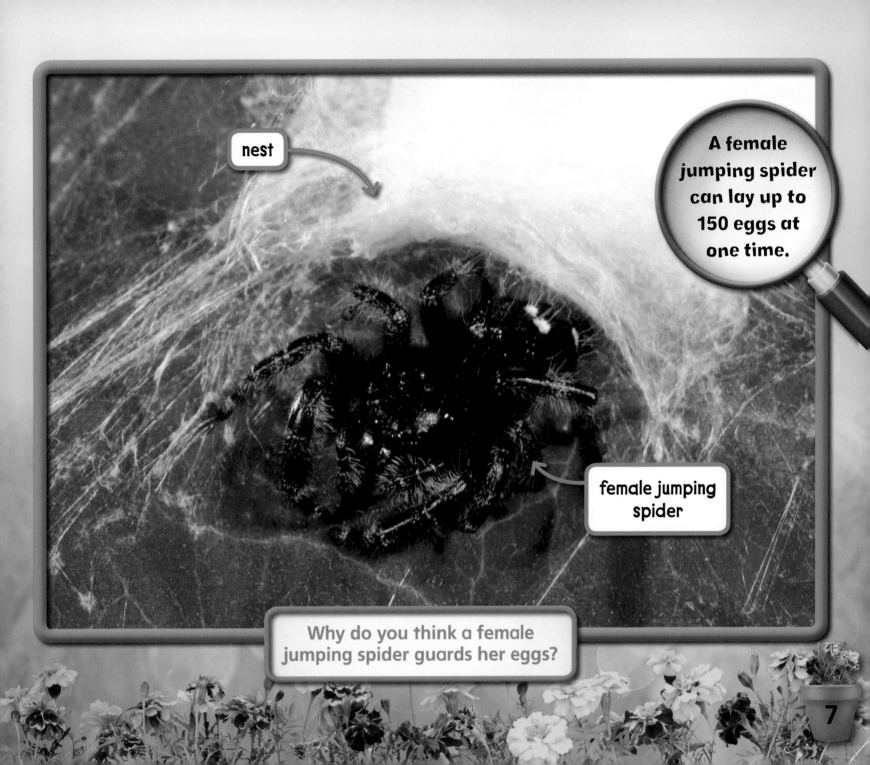

nest

A female jumping spider can lay up to 150 eggs at one time.

female jumping spider

Why do you think a female jumping spider guards her eggs?

Date: July 6

The Babies Hatch

The female spider guards her eggs to stop other spiders and **insects** from eating them.

After three weeks, tiny baby spiders called spiderlings hatched from the eggs.

At first, the babies stayed inside their egg sac.

Today, the two-week-old babies climbed out of the nest.

They ran around on the porch and scampered off into the backyard.

spiderlings

If 16 baby jumping spiders stood together in a line, it would measure just one inch (2.5 cm) long.

a close-up view of spiderlings in a nest

Date: July 7

Leaving Home

When one of the tiny spiderlings left home, it released a thin silk strand into the air.

One end was attached to its body.

When a breeze blew, the baby spider was lifted into the air.

It floated out into the yard like a tiny kite and landed on the grass.

silk strand

spiderling

a close-up view of a spiderling

A mother jumping spider does not take care of her babies once they leave the egg sac.

Imagine you are talking to a friend who has never seen a baby jumping spider. Describe to your friend what the spiderling looks like.

Date: __September 1__

A New Exoskeleton

The spiderlings are ten weeks old, and they are growing bigger and hairier.

Today, one of the babies in the yard split out of its exoskeleton.

As a spider grows bigger, its outer covering stays the same size so it gets too tight.

When a spider bursts out of its old exoskeleton, there's a new, bigger one underneath!

new exoskeleton

old exoskeleton

When a spider sheds its exoskeleton, it's called molting. A jumping spider molts about five times before it is fully grown.

a spiderling on a leaf

Date: **October 22**

Spotting a Meal

The spiders are four months old—and they are almost fully grown.

The fast-moving hunters have been catching insects since they left the egg sac.

Their eight eyes help them become very good at hunting.

A jumping spider uses its two big front eyes to spot **prey** and figure out how far away it is.

It uses the eyes on the side of its head to spot a meal off to one side!

Jumping spiders eat flies, crickets, and other insects. They also eat spiders.

14

Jump for It

Today, I spotted a jumping spider and an insect called a leafhopper on a plant.

Even though it was several inches away from the leafhopper, the spider pounced!

As it jumped, a little silk strand came out of its body.

The spider had attached one end of the strand to the plant before it jumped.

A jumping spider can jump up to 50 times the length of its body!

leafhopper

jumping spider

silk strand

Why do you think the spider makes a silk strand when it pounces on its prey?

Date: __October 24__

Time for Dinner

If a jumping spider misses its jump, it can climb back up its strand and try again.

Today, I saw a spider make a huge leap to catch a fly.

The spider grabbed the fly and quickly bit into it with its sharp **fangs**.

The spider used its fangs to give the fly a shot of poison called venom.

The venom made the fly unable to move, so the spider could eat it.

fangs

Spiders spit up juices from their stomachs onto their food. The juices help to make the food soft enough for the spider to eat.

jumping spider

fly

Date: **December 5**

Waiting for Spring

Some of the spiders that hatched on our porch are now making nests.

Winter is here, and the cold weather could kill them.

However, their little silk homes will keep the spiders safe and warm.

When spring comes, they will be adults and ready to mate.

I can't wait to see the spiders dancing and laying eggs again!

nest

There are about 5,000 different kinds of jumping spiders around the world.

The spiders in this book are known as bold, or daring, jumping spiders. Why do you think people gave them these names?

Giant Jumps

A jumping spider can jump up to 50 times the length of its body!

How far can you jump?

Lie down on the floor and have a friend cut a piece of string or yarn that is as long as you are.

Next, choose a spot to start from, and then jump as far as you can.

Place something on the ground to show where you landed.

Measure your jump using the string.

Did you jump farther than the length of your body?

Science Words

exoskeleton
(*eks*-oh-SKEL-uh-tuhn)
the hard covering that
protects the bodies of
some kinds of animals, such
as insects and spiders

fangs (FANGZ) long, sharp
teeth used for holding
prey, or injecting prey
with venom

insects (IN-sekts) small
animals that have six
legs, an exoskeleton, two
antennas, and three main
body parts

mate (MAYT) to come
together in order to have
young

prey (PRAY) an animal
that is hunted by other
animals for food

silk (SILK) a soft, shiny
thread that is made
by some insects and
spiders

Index

Read More

Goldish, Meish. *Jumping Spiders (No Backbone!).* New York: Bearport (2009).

Marsh, Laura. *Spiders.* Washington, D.C.: National Geographic (2011).

Robbins, Lynette. *Jumping Spiders (Jump!).* New York: PowerKids Press (2012).

Learn More Online

To learn more about jumping spiders, visit **www.bearportpublishing.com/AnimalDiaries**

About the Author

Ellen Lawrence lives in the United Kingdom. Her favorite books to write are those about animals. In fact, the first book Ellen bought for herself, when she was six years old, was the story of a gorilla named Patty Cake that was born in New York's Central Park Zoo.

1